CONTENTS

Introduction to Estuary English	3
Dictionary of Estuary English	7
Recipes	57
The Cockney alphabet	61

Airpiece
See page 8

Dijja Wanna Say Sumfing?

A guide to
Estuary English

Steve Crancher

Illustrated by
Ash

Ian Henry Publications

ISBN 0 86025 534 4

All characters in this book are fictitious
and any similarity to persons
living or dead
is entirely coincidental

Published by
Ian Henry Publications, Ltd.,
20 Park Drive, Romford, Essex RM1 4LH
Printed by
ColourBooks, Ltd., Dublin, 13, Ireland

Introduction

Linguists have been discussing Estuary English since - and probably even before - the term was coined in 1984 by David Rosewarne. At the time, Rosewarne was involved in linguistic research at Birkbeck College, London, and his article in the *Times Educational Supplement* described the accent/dialect as ‘a variety of modified regional speech’.

It is generally considered that Estuary English is somewhere on a continuum between Received Pronunciation (BBC or Queen’s English) and cockney. However, while the Hooray Henrys (the young upper class) of the 1980s have long since adopted it in an effort to gain some street credibility, the majority of people think of Estuary English as that used by Essex Man and Essex Woman (from towns in the south of the county) - that is, the part of the continuum closer to cockney than to Received Pronunciation. This is, perhaps, real Estuary English - what this book is all about.

Estuary English existed long before 1984, but gathered pace in the 1980s. This was a time when television companies embraced regional dialects rather than teach us all how to be better citizens. In 1985 the BBC launched the soap opera *EastEnders*, and Australian soaps such as

Neighbours had a big influence on children and teenagers.

No probs, mate. No worries.

Also in the 1980s the stock exchange was deregulated and new traders began to sound more like East End market traders than the traditional financial market tones of Received Pronunciation.

The mixture of these various influences on the South East accent has probably resulted in Estuary English.

Television continues to have an effect with new words and phrases arriving from America, and being readily accepted by youngsters. With transport links and television, features of Estuary English can now be heard as far north as Leeds and Manchester, and west to Bristol.

Estuary English is spreading fast.

So what are the features of Estuary English? The first and most obvious is the pronunciation of the letter **T**. In general this has been replaced by a glottal stop, except when it occurs at the beginning of a word. The Received Pronunciation speaker will tap the T, *i.e.* pronounce it distinctly. The Estuary English speaker will drop the T (this is the glottal stop) especially when followed by another consonant. A common example is the word Gatwick. With the glottal stop it becomes Ga'wick. There is pronunciation though; for example there is a difference between the words beat and be.

However, when the T is followed by a vowel sound, the T is not always dropped. In the sentence, 'Are you going to the football on Saturday?', the T in football will be replaced by a glottal stop, while Saturday may well see the T tapped.

Th is commonly replaced by **F** at the beginning of a syllable, or **V** if it occurs elsewhere. 'I think my brother's rather stupid' would be 'I fink my bruvver's fick'.

H is also dropped at the beginning of a syllable. So 'Hello Harry' becomes 'Allo Arry'.

L is pronounced with a **W** sound, and Estuary English speakers will probably not be aware of this. For example, hill becomes hiw.

Finally, the vowel sound **ou**, or **ow**, becomes a slightly extended **a** sound, although at the normal rate of speech this does not always occur. The extended **a** sound is over-emphasised when taken out of a sentence, but 'the couch is in the lounge' is written and pronounced simply as 'the cach is in the lange'. To make this clearer within the text the long **a** sound is indicated by a pair of bars **ā̃** over the letter.

The main characters used in examples of words and phrases are: Darren and Tracey, a couple aged between 25 and

35; their son Jordan, aged between 3 and 14; Tracey's friend Sharon; Darren's friends Dave and Craig; Jordan's friend Connor; Tracey's mum; and Aunt Cathy. Entries are written as pronounced at the rate of speech.

<u>Underlining denotes emphasis</u>

tt = teenage terminology
sl = slang

Fermals
See page 26

Chiz to the following:

Ian Wilkes, Greg Fidgeon, Rob Mellett, Lisa Mundy, Bobs, Claire, Graeme, Kerry, Andy, Steve, Jerome, Dave, Keef, Rosemary, Irene, Sid, John, Ben, Lewis, Reece and Mitch, Deb, Mick, Ciddy, Ashley, Darren, Trace, Jordan & co., Pete and Tab from Fives.

A

a cutla two (*'Do us a cutla slices o' toast, wilya sweetart.'*)

a cutla quid a small, unspecified amount of money (*'I won a cutla quid on the awsses.'*)

abãt 1) on the subject of (*'Wot yer talking abat, Trace?'*); 2) approximately (*'The geezer in the garrij reckons it'll be abat 200 quid.'*)

accãnt an arrangement with a shop for credit (*'I got an accant at the bookies.'*)

ack

in football, to tackle a player with no regard for his well being or the ball (*'Gawon, Jordan, ack im dan.'*)

addit no longer functional *(Oi, Trace, I fink the motah's addit.')*

afflete a person with natural physical ability (*'Ere, Sharon, your Connor's a bit of an afflete, innee.'*)

ag *sl.* an ugly, usually old, woman (*'Shut it, you old ag.'*)

ai? I beg your pardon? (*'Ere, Trace, why doancha try not bleaching yer air this time?' 'Ai?'*)

airbrush a grooming accessory for smoothing the hair (*'I didden know what to say next so I it im wiv the airbrush.'*)

airdo style of a woman's hair (*'Like yer new airdo, Trace.' 'Chiz, mate.'*)

airpiece wig

airy alarming (*'Blimey, that was a bit airy.'*)

ake *sl.* (usually **the ake**) upset. Also **right ake** – well upset (*'Oi, look; Tracy's got the right ake wiv Darren.'*)

alâd permitted (*'My Jordan's alad to do anyfing he wants.'*)
all saffisticated educated, refined, cultured (*'Ere, Darren, you got all saffisticated since ya went to Saff Kensinton.'*)
allway a passage beyond the front door of a house (*'Darren, shwee do up the allway?'*)
alma chizzit what does it cost?
amânt quantity; sum total (*'Thez a yuge amant of mud at Saffend.'*)
am sanwij a snack consisting of two slices of bread with a piece of pig meat between, often served wiv mustard or pickle – luvverly
amma

a tool used for banging nails in (*'Janoe ow to use an amma, Jordan?'*)
ampa a box of food saved for all year to eat at Christmas (*'This year we're getting an ampa wiv salmon innit.'*)
amsta rodent pet that keeps you awake all night long (*'We got Jordan an amsta for iz burfdee.'*)

an'all also (*'Yeh, Dave, I got a Fiesta an'all.'*)
anbag a bag that a woman carries around, famously and mythically holding everything but the kitchen sink
and 1) the end of the arm beyond the wrist; 2) assistance (*'Oi, Darren, give us an and, wilya?'*)
andalwit cope (*'Thass the job; ja fink ya can andalwit?'*)
andy *sl.* useful; capable (*'My Jordan's well andy wiv iz fists.'*)
anfem a song with a rousing chorus
angover

an eddake caused by drinking too much alcohol (*'Not now, Darren; I got an angover.'*)
anight this evening; this night (*'Ja fancy goan at anight, sweetart?'*)
anky a piece of material carried about primarily to sneeze into or blow one's nose on
anky-panky *sl.* naughtiness

annee has he not (*'Jordan's bin a bit better this munf, annee Trace.'*)

annuvva an additional; one more (*'...And if yer not careful I'll give yer annuvva one.'*)

ansom *sl.* very nice; very good (*'These arf pandas are ansom.'*)

apafy lack of interest

appy burfdee many happy returns of the day

ard 1) firm and solid (*'Trace, this bread pudding you made is ard as anyfing.'*); 2) difficult; 3) tough (*'I'm well ard, me.'*)

arf 1) the floor of the fireplace; 2) equal parts of a whole; 3) half a pint of beer (*'Dave's on the arfs tonight.'*)

arf pãnda a well big hamburger

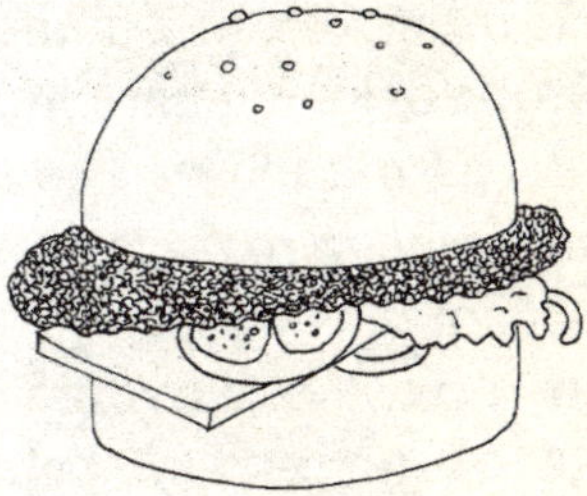

arfryetus pain and stiffness of the joints (*'Me arfryetus is playing me up again.'*)

aright? hello

ark at listen to (*'Ark at you wiv all yer airs an' graces.'*)

arm 1) upper limb starting at the shoulder; 2) hurt, injure (*'It don't do ya no arm.'*)

arsed *sl.* bothered (usually used in negative, as in *'I can't be arsed.'*)

arst past tense of ask *('Jordan, I must've arst ya free fuzzund times to clear up yer room.')*

art the organ of the body that pumps blood

art attack *sl.* extemely perturb (*'Don't tell Sharon, she'll av an art attack.'*)

art set covet (*'Jordan ad iz art set on that scooter.'*)

ẫss a structure used as a home (*'I'm doing me ass up.'*)

Ẫssa Commons Parliament building

ẫssbẫnd unable to leave the house because of illness, disability, etc

ẫssusband male version of asswife

ẫsswife woman who does cooking, cleaning, etc, in a home

ẫsswork regular chores done by asswife or assusband (*'Darren, can we get someone in to do the asswork?'*)

ẫt not in

at a piece of cloving worn on the nut (qv)

ẫt of order *sl.* behaving in a manner contrary to one's peers (*'Oi, Darren, you're at of order.'*)

ẫtbreak a sudden eruption (*'Yer avving an atbreak of nuttiness today, Trace' 'Yeh, I fink I'm due on.'*)

ẫtburst explosion of anger

ẫtdo surpass; *past tense* **ẫtdun** (*'Eez atdun ya, annee.'*)

ẫtdoors the garden of a house (*'Iss a beautiful day, Darren; less go atdoors.'*)

ate intense dislike (*'I ate cabbage, me.'*)

ãtfit a set of clothes worn together (*'Thass a nice atfit, Sharon.' 'Chiz, mate.'*)

ãtraijus shocking (*'Oi, Sharon, your roots are atraijus.'*)

ãtside the external side or surface; in the open air (*'Jordan, why doancha go atside for a bit.'*)

ãttin an excursion

avvac confusion and disorder (*'This Spanish grub's playing avvac wiv me innards.'*)

awd an amassed store (*'Craig's got an awd of cash under iz mattress.'*)

awfa a writer of books (*'So you fink yer an awfa do ya?'*)

awfentic genuine; realistic (*'I love that movie Braivart cos it's got Mel Gibson in it an it's well awfentic.'*)

awforities political or administrative bodies with delegated power

awfority delegated power

awss a four-legged animal, upon which money is won and, more likely, lost (*'That awss you tipped cost me a fiver today.'*)

Awton Tãz a large theme park

ãz that which belongs to us (*'This villa is all az for the week.'*)
ãzzit 1) how is it (*azzit going?*); 2) how does it (*azzit work?*); 3) has it

B

backander

a secret payment, usually delivered in a brown envelope
bagga criss a bag containing flavoured potato snacks (*'Oi, Jordan, wojja ave for yer lunch today?' 'A bagga criss an' a canna coke.'*)
ballistic *sl.* mad with rage (*'I better get ome or Trace'll go ballistic.'*)
bananas *sl.* an under-fives football team, so called because the players run around in bunches
bãnce cause to rebound
baneef 1) below; 2) not worthy of (*'I don't do washing up, Darren; it's baneef me.'*)

bang ẫt of order *sl.* see *at of order*

bẫnnsa

a person employed to deny access or eject troublemakers at a club (*'Dave's got izself a job as a bannsa.'*)

bẫnta certainly will (*'Ere, Trace, drekkun Craig will like me new fong?' 'Eez banta.'*)

Bẫnty a chocolate and coconut snack bar

bare /tt/ very (*'Ere, Jordan, thass a bare phat cap ya got on.'*)

barf

a large container in which one bathes (*'Oi, Darren, when was the last time you ad a barf?'*)

bave to wash oneself

be'ave conduct oneself properly (*'Jordan, you better be'ave yerself at yer Aunt Caffy's.'*)
be'ind 1) to the rear of; 2) the posterior
bell call on a telephone (*'gissa bell'*)
bettern'i (*Literal translation – better hadn't I*) I ought (*'I'll ave t' buy yer a pint then, bettern'i.')*
big time/big style *sl.* plentifully (*'It wennoff big style.'*)
bin 1) past participle of be (*'Where the ell av you bin till this time o' night?'*); 2) *sl.* a place to keep money – pocket, purse, wallet, jam jar, bank account, etc. (*'Eeyar Jordan, stick this jacks in yer bin.' 'Chiz dad.'*)
bitta dinna meal, usually evening (*'Oi, Darren, ja fancy a bitta dinna?*)
bladdered *sl.* very, very drunk (*'I was well bladdered last night.'*)
blag 1) *sl.* exaggerate; lie; 2) *sl.* borrow, usually surreptitiously
blinding *sl.* excellent (*'West Am scored a blinding goal yesterday.'*)

bling /tt/ cool new acquisition (*'Oi, Connor, ya seen me bling cell?'*)

blower *sl.* telephone (*'Quick, Dave, get on the blower and see if ya can do the 4 dog at Romford.'*)

boaf the two (*'Oi, Dave, ooja fancy most, Sharon or Tracey?' 'Boaf.'*)

the bookies bookmaker; turf accountant

boot boot sale (*'Ere Dave, ya goan dan the boot Sunday?'*)

borra acquire temporarily with the intention of returning (*'Ere, Dave, can I borra yer motuh?'*)

bort purchased (*'I bort it from a geezer dan the juicer.'*)

bottle *sl.* courage (*'You ain't got the bottle.'*)

bovva to trouble; worry (*'Don't bovva me now, Jordan; can't ya see I'm watching the box?'*)

box *sl.* television

brãn colour, like chocolate or shade thereof

brãnna more brown than at a previous time (*'Ere, Trace, you look branna today.' 'Yeh, I've bin under the sunbed.'*)
Bransatch motor racing circuit in Kent
breave to take breaths
breff air taken into or expelled from the lungs
brew *sl.* cup of tea (*'Ere, Trace, ja fancy making a brew?'*)
brilyant very good
bruvver male sibling
bung give (*'Bung us a pony and I'll sawt it for ya.'*)
burfdee boy / burfdee gell the person celebrating a burfdee
burfdee day commemorating a person's birth, often celebrated

C

cãch

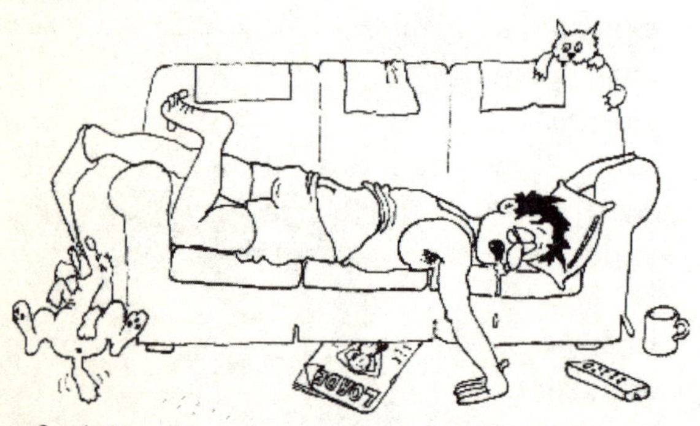

sofa (*'I'm knackered; I fink I'll lay on the cach for a bit.'*)
caf eating house open during the day
Caffy a girl's name

cãncel administrative body of a town, district, etc (*'Darren, wiv ad annuvva letter from the cancel.'*)
cãnt repeat numbers in ascending order (*'Ere, guess what? Jordan can cant up to an undred.'*)
cãntafit fake
cãntdãn repeat numbers in descending order to zero
cãnter a long surface in a shop, café, etc, over which business is conducted
cãnty a large administrative area incorporating towns, villages, etc. (eg Essex)
cell /tt/ mobile phone
cheers thank you
chiz *alternative of cheers* (*'Chiz for that, mate.'*)
choker *sl.* an unfortunate or disappointing outcome (*'They equalised in the 91st minute – what a choker.'*)
choon good song
choona an edible fish purchased in a tin and usually prepared with mayonnaise
chuck throw (*'Ere, Trace, chuck us the remote.'*)
chuck up *sl.* to vomit (*'I fink I'm gonna chuck up.'*)
chuffed *sl.* happy
chunda *sl.* to vomit (*'I fink I'm gonna chunda.'*)

cl̃ãddy overcast
cl̃ãt a blow (*'Oi, Jordan, pack it in or I'll give yer a clat rand the ear.'*)
cloff woven material
clove to put on clothes
cloze garments worn on the body (*'Darren, I'm goan dan tan t' get some new cloze.'*)
clump hit; strike (usually non-aggressive threat to child, as in *'Jordan, you do that again and I'll clump yer.'*)
come a (right) cropper *sl.* experience a disappointing or painful outcome (*'I come a right cropper dan the bookies today.'*)

cop *sl.* good (usually used with negative prefix to indicate something not good, as in *'This video's not much cop.'*)
cort past tense of catch (*'I fink I cort a cold.'*)
cort a pãnda a big hamburger (*see* arf panda)
cos because
crack (one) up *sl.* amuse (*'Oi, Darren, you really crack me up.'*)
cract it succeeded (*'I fink you've cract it, son.'*)

crãd

a large group of people (*'There was a good crad at West Am yesterday.'*)

crãn what the Queen wears on her nut

D

d'narf very much (*'Oi Darren, your feet d'narf stink.'*)

dammij *sl.* cost (*'Chiz, guv; wot's the dammij?'*)

dãn 1) towards a lower place; 2) to (*'I'm goan dan the juicer.'*)

dãn ill 1) in the direction to the bottom of an incline; 2) deteriorate (*'Aunt Caffy's gone a bit dan ill lately.'*)

dãn in the mãff unhappy (*'What's up, Trace; ya look a bit dan in the maff.'*)

dãn tãn to the tansenter (*'I'm goan dan tan.'*)

dãn the pan of no further use; worse than previously
dãn to urf sensible; practical
dãnload To transfer information, music, etc, from the internet to a computer
Dãnning Street where the prime minister lives
dãnstez where the biggest telly is
dãt uncertain (*'Sorry, Trace, but I dat Jordan's gonna be a rocket scientist.'*)
decent /tt/ good
deff the ending of life (*'Oi, Darren, you'll be the deff o' me.'*)
denãnce condemn (*'Darren, I denance ya.' 'You wot?'*)
didden did not
dijja did you (*'Dijja wanna say sumfing?'*)
dint did not
dintya did you not (*'Dintya wanna go on the school trip, Jordan?'*)
diss *sl.* speak ill of (short for disrespect)
divva 1) be indecisive (*'Come on, Jordan, don't divva.'*); 2) a state of agitation (*'I'm all of a divva.'*)
do the offs! /tt/ run away!
do wot? I beg your pardon? (*'Ere, Trace, why doancha try not bovvrin wiv make-up?' 'Do wot?'*)
doan do not (*'Ya doan 'ave t' go if ya doan wanna.'*)
doancha do you not (*'Oi, Darren, doancha like me anymore?'*)
doddle *sl.* a simple task

dodgy *sl.* dubious person or thing (*'Eez a dodgy geezer.'*)
done rubbish performed badly *(Jordan, ya doen rubbish at yer exams.' 'Chiz, dad.')*
donut *sl.* idiot (*'Leave it at, Jordan, you donut.'*)
drãn kill by submersion in liquid
drãndid killed by submersion in liquid
drãzzy half asleep; sluggish (*'I'm all drazzy after that wine.'*)
drekkun do you consider (*'Which dog drekkun'll win the next race?'*)

E

ear 1) to listen to; *past tense* **urd** (*'Yeh alright, I can ear ya.'*)
earake an excuse for telling someone to quieten down (*'Givvit a rest, wilya; yer givin me earake.'*)
earbashin to talk incessantly (*'Sharon's givin im a right old earbashin.'*)
eassbãnd in an easterly direction
eat 1) consume food; 2) condition of being hot (*'Trace, me dinner's cold; can you eat it up for us.'*)
eave 1) rise and fall rhythmically; 2) throw
ed the uppermost part of the body, above the neck
eddake continuous discomfort or pain in the head (*'Not now, Darren; I got eddake.'*)

eel 1) the back part of the foot; 2) command to dog to walk close to its owner

eeva one or the other (*'Eeva 'e goes or I go.'*)

eeyar there you are (when giving) (*'Eeyar, mate, stick this in yer bin.'*)

eez 1) he is; 2) belonging to him (alt. spelling of iz) (*'E ain't no oil painting but av you seen eez bird?'*)

effix moral principals (*'That Dave ain't got no effix.'*)

efty considerable (*'Ere, Trace, this credit card bill's a bit efty.'*)

ejog

a small, spiky mammal

elf the state of being fit and well (*'Just be grateful you've still got your elf, young man.'*)

enfewsiastic eager (*'Blimey, you're enfewsiastic, intya?'*)

ennyfing a thing of any kind; *alt spelling* **ennyfink** (*'Darren, is there ennyfink wrong?'*)

ere 1) in or at this place (*'What you doing ere?'*); 2) *as a prefix*, listen to this (*'Ere, Darren, you urd the one abat the free-legged nun?'*)

erz belonging to her

essdree the tidal mouth of a river

evva an ericaceous shrub, said to be lucky and hawked by old women in the tansenter to mugs (qv)

evvy 1) of great weight; 2) a big geezer who protects a smaller and more intelligent geezer, usually for money (*'My name's Frank and this is me evvy, Knuckles.'*)

evvy-anded clumsy (*'Darren, jafta be so evvy-anded?'*)

eyebrow cultured, intellectual (*'Mar cousin's a bit eyebrow.'*)

eye-eels women's shoes

F

fãnd discovered (*'Oi, Jordan, where ja get that video recorder?' 'I fand it.'*)

fãntin a jet of water for drinking or ornament

fanx an expression of gratitude

farva *posh way of saying* dad

Fatcha Margaret – British Prime Minister 1979-1990

faw to return something frozen to its unfrozen state

fawd past tense of faw (*'I doan fink the turkey's fawd.'*)

fãzzund In maths, 10x100; 1,000

feef a person who steals

feem subject or topic

feem park an amusement park

feem pub a public house decorated and furnished around a specific idea

fee'eta a building for dramatic performance

feery speculative thought (*'My feery is it's run at of petrol.'*)

feev steal; nick

feft act of thieving

fermals heat-retaining undergarments worn in cold weather

fermastat a device to regulate temperature, or activate another device at a certain temperature

ferrapy non-surgical treatment of physical or mental disorders

fick 1) stupid (*'Darren, are you being fick on purpose?'*); 2) a liquid firm in consistency (*'This milk shake's well fick.'*); 3) of great extent between surfaces (*'This wall's free feet fick.'*)

fiff position number 5 in a sequence, written thus: 5th

filfy dirty; rude (*'Leave it at, you filfy sod.'*)

fin 1) a liquid of slight consistency (*'This milk shake's well fin.'*); 2) opposite surfaces close together (*'These walls are paper fin.'*)

fing 1) object; 2) idea, problem, action (*'The fing is, wot we gonna do abat it?'*)

fingy a person or object whose name doesn't come to mind (*'I ad it off wiv fingy last night.'*)

fink ponder (*'I can't fink wiv all this racket.'*)

fit attractive (*'Oi, Sharon, you seen that geezer in Pandland? Eez well fit.'*)

follad frew *sl.* had an accident in one's pants (*'That one's well bad – I fink you must've follad frew.'*)

follerin behind; support (*'Orient ad a decent follerin at West Am at the weekend.'*)

fong skimpy undergarment

for cryin ẫt lẫd mild expletive showing annoyance or surprise (*For cryin at lad, Jordan; if I say yes will you give it a rest?'*)

forff position number 4 in a sequence, written thus: 4th

Forp Park a large theme park

fort past tense of fink (*'I fort you woz at.'*)

fortful meditative

fortless careless of consequences or others' feelings

fotas pictures (*'Av a look at me olladay fotas.'*)

frãn pulling together of eyebrows, denoting concentration or anger (*'Oi, Jordan, wipe that fran off yer face.'*)

France a place where booze and smokes are cheap

frash defeat thoroughly in a game or contest (*'We frashed ya.'*)

fred pass cotton, ribbon, etc, through a hole or series of holes (*'Fred it froo.'*); a piece of cotton or similar

fredbare worn out

free in maffs, the number between 2 and 4, thus: 3

freefinka a person who doesn't wear a baseball cap

freek meyãt worry me (*'You really freek meyat.'*)

fret declaration of intention to hurt (*'Is that some sort o' fret?'*)
fretten make a threat
frifty financially economical (*'Darren, you can be well frifty sometimes.'*)
frill

excited emotion
frilla an exciting film
frive flourish
froat the front part of the neck; the windpipe (*'Ere, Trace, Dave's ad a tattoo dun on iz froat; I fink I'll get one.'*)
frob pulsate (*'E it iz fum wiv the amma and now it's frobbin.'*)
fro propel through the air (*'As it's yer burfdee we're gonna fro ya in the river.'*)

froff top part of a pint of beer, a cappuccino or a freshly poured fizzy drink

frone 1) a chair on which the Queen sits when she is working; 2) the lavatory (*'Wez the paipa?; I'm goana sit on the frone.'*)

froo 1) past tense of froe (*'Oo froo that?'*); 2) going in one end or side and out the other (*'Ere look, Jordan, we're goan froo the Dartford Tunnel.'*)

frottle 1) a pedal or lever operating the speed of a vehicle; accelerate (*'Gawon, Dave, give it some frottle.'*); 2) choke

fudd a low, dull sound (*'Did you just ear a fudd?'*)

fug hooligan (*'My Jordan may be many fings but 'e ain't no fug.'*)

fum a digit on the hand (*'Trace, I just smacked me fum wiv the amma.'*)

fump strike (*'I'll give ya a fump if you ain't careful.'*)

funder loud noise when lightning strikes

furd position number 3 in a sequence, written thus: 3rd

furra complete

Furrock the area where Lakeside is

fursty feeling in need of a drink

fye the upper part of the leg (*'Me fye's all tingly.'*)

G

gaff *sl* house; home (*'So, geezer, ja wanna come an avva gander at me gaff?'*)

gander look

garrij a place in which a car is kept or repaired (*Trace: 'Sorry Darren, I fink the motah needs to go in the garrij; I pranged it when I was parking.'*)

gawon go on (*'Gawon, Jordan, eat ya granny's cabbidge - it won't do ya no arm.'*)

geddin there 1) attempt 2) join in 3) victorious exclamation *('Ere, Darren, I fink we won a tenner on the lottery.' 'Geddin there!')*

geezer a man

geezer bird a masculine woman; a tomboy

get ere come hither (command to a dog or child)

gissa bell contact on a telephone

give it a rest a request to discontinue speech or action (*'Give it a rest, wilya?'*)

give it large to be thorough or enthusiastic

go spare become distraught (*'For cryin at lad, Jordan, I'm goan spare wiv you.'*)

goan ẫt leaving the house

goana going to (a place)

goana grẫnd to go into hiding

gob mouth

gobsmacked *sl* flabberghasted

goes said (*'...So he just goes "wait and see, Trace".'*)

gonna 1) going to (do something); 2) a person doomed

gotcha got you

grẫnd 1) the earth's surface; 2) a football stadium (*'It all wennoff atside the pub near the grand.'*)

grand £1,000 sterling

grẫndid to a child, confined to the home as punishment (*'Jordan, if ya do that again yer grandid.'*)

grub food

guess what? unanswerable and rhetorical question often used as a prelude to the announcement of news (*'Guess what? Jordan's gone up annuvva shoe size.'*)

gutted upset

H

haitch letter of the alphabet between G and I

I

Ibeefa Balearic holiday island

iffy dubious (*'Ere, Trace, I fink this bread pudding you made last munf's a bit iffy.'*)

inj a mechanism upon which a door is hung

innee is he not

innit 1) is it not; 2) *superfluous suffix* (*'I'm goana Romford tansenter, innit.'*)

int indirect suggestion (*'I gave Darren a sort of int that it was time to wash iz feet.'*)

intshee is she not
intya are you not
ips an unknown area of a woman's body to which chocolate travels (*'That Mars Bar will go straight to me ips.'*)
iss it is (*'Iss a well nice day today.'*)
isstry 1) past events; 2) no longer involved in a particular activity (*'Eez isstry.'*)
it strike (*'Gawon, Jordan, it it.'*)
itched married (*'Craig's getting itched, the muppet.'*)
itchike

travel by means of thumbing a lift
iz belonging to him (*'That's iz, that is.'*)
izself himself (*'Ere, look at Craig – eez well chuffed wiv izself.'*)

ja do you; did you (*'Ja like me new airdo, Darren?'*)

jacks *sl* five pound note (*'Lend us a jacks, wilya.'*)

jafta? Is it really necessary? (shows mild annoyance) (*'Oi, Darren, jafta keep doing that?'*)

jamember do you remember (*'Jamember when Jordan woz little?'*)

jammy *sl* lucky (*'That Craig's a right jammy sod.'*)

janartamean do you know what I mean (sometimes used as nartamean)

janoe do you know

jarmas loose fitting clothes worn in bed (*'Get yer jarmas on, Jordan.'*)

jaw talk incessantly (*'When them wimmin get togevva they d'narf jaw.'*)

jawler a shop that sells jewellery (*'Ere, Darren, less go dan the jawlers for an eternity ring.'*)

jawls precious stones (*'Yeh, iss well nice, but how many jawls as it got?'*)

jicer a substance in a pressurised can used for melting ice from the windscreen of a motor vehicle (*'Oi, Trace, the motah's all snowed up - wejja put the jicer?'*)

juicer *sl.* pub (*'You bin dan that juicer again, Darren?'*)

just the job perfect (*'That pint was just the job.'*)

jyenormous extremely large

K

kebab grub consisting of meat, salad, and lashings of chilli sauce in pitta bread eaten after leaving a pub or club when one has the munchies (qv)

L

lãd very noisy (*'Oi, Jordan, turn that pony dan, it's too lad.'*)

bit of a lad – mischievous boy or youth

lafarjik lacking in energy (*'I feel all lafarjik today.'*)

lame /tt/ of poor quality or taste (*'Yer cell's well lame, Connor.'*)

lãnge room in a house where the telly is

larf sound expressing amusement or derision; **avving a larf** – not serious (*'Yer avving a larf.'*); messing about

larj (**livin it larj**) enjoying oneself; (**larjing it (up)**) blagging (qv)

larva froth from soap and water

leave it ãt 1) please desist (*'Oi, leave it at.'*); 2) disagree

leggit

run away

less let us (*'Darren, less go at anight, eh?'*)

levva material made from the skin of an animal

lippy outspoken

liquid lunch a break in the middle of the day spent drinking alcohol (*'I ad a liquid lunch today; I'm well mullered.'*)

lock in in a pub, drinking after hours

lotree costs a pound for a ticket

lyebree 1) a public building housing books for use of the public (*'Guess what, Darren; videos are n'arf cheap dan the lyebree.'*) 2) male word for the lavatory (*'Wez the paipa?; I wanna go t' the lyebree.'*)

M

Ma Blarch an arch in Hyde Park

mẫff gob;

maffs the study of numbers

mãffy outspoken
mãnd a small hill
Mand a girl's name
manor local area
mãnt get up on (a horse) (*'Are ya gonna mant that awss or wot?'*)
mãntin a large natural elevation of the Urf's surface
mãntneerin the sport of climbing mantins
mar my (when emphasised) (*'Eez not your bloke, eez mar bloke.'*) see also **me**
mãss a small rodent (*'Oi, Darren, I fink thez a mass be'ind the fridge.'*)
me my (*'Wez me pint gone?'*)
meffs meffylated spirit
miff 1) offend; 2) a fictitious person or thing. **urban miff**: a widely held but false notion

mijit a very small person or thing
minger an unattractive person (usually woman)
minnit an unspecific period of time (*'I'll give yer a bell back in a minnit.'*)
mischeevious mischievous

moff flying nocturnal insect attracted to light
monkey *sl.* five hundred pounds sterling
moody /tt/ poor quality; rubbish (*'Oi, Connor, wejja get ya moody trainers?'*)
motah car (usually Ford Fiesta)
mug *sl.* a naïve person (*'Eez a bit of a mug.'*)
mullered *sl.* very, very drunk
mullwill a small mound made by a mole when burrowing. **make a mãntin at of a mullwill**: exaggerate a minor difficulty
munchies (usually **the munchies**) peckishness or hunger brought on by the exertions of an evening out (*'I got the munchies – less go dan the kebab shop.'*)
munf period approximately equivalent to the moon's rotation around the Earth
muppet *sl.* idiot
muvva female parent

N

narra lacking breadth; with little margin (*'Darren, my mum wannid to come rand but she changed er mind' 'That woz a narra escape, Trace.'*)
nart sympathy (*'Av a nart, Trace.'*)
nartamean do you know what I mean (sometimes used as janartamean)
nasty niff an offensive odour
nãdays in these times; at present *('Aunt Caff said everyfings different nadays.')*
naya this very moment *('Get ere naya!')*

Neanderfull

a person who shows a lack of understanding of modern life (*'Darren, you can be a right Neanderfull sometimes.'*)

neeva not one nor the other (*Wojja want – cabbij or Brussels sprats?' 'Neeva.'*)

nessry required; essential (*'Is that really nessry?'*)

never did not (*'You said you woz goan at.' 'No I never.'*)

NHS National Elf Service

nice wun congratulations (*'I won a monkey on the lotree.' 'Nice wun.'*)

no wurriz 1) never mind; 2) you're welcome (*'Chiz for that, mate.' 'No wurriz.'*)

norfbãnd in a northerly direction

norff a direction of the compass (opp: saff)

nuffing 1) not a thing; 2) anything (*'I ain't dun nuffing.'*)

nuffing much to shãt abãt not particularly special (*'Ya seen Craig's new bird?' 'Yeh; nuffing much to shat abat.'*)

nuffink alternative of nuffing

nugget *sl* a one pound coin sterling

nut 1) head; 2) *in football*, to strike the ball with the head (*'I keep putting crosses in but you ain't nutting em in.'*)

nutta a person prone to outrageous or aggressive behaviour, esp when drunk (*'Eez a right nutta.'*)

nutmeg in football, to kick the ball through the legs of an opposing player

nuttiness irrational behaviour

O

oaf a solemn declaration of truth or commitment

off one's nut intoxicated with alcohol

oi excuse me

oi oi! Traditional greeting in pub, usually uttered from across the room

ol an aperture; a gap (*'I got an ol in me trainer'*)

olladay time taken away from home for rest, adventure, etc, often abroad

ome the place where you live (*'Oi, Dave, ain't you got an ome to go to?'*)
one a one pound coin (*'As anybody got five ones for a jacks?'*)
onnist fair and just; without a lie (*'I never did it, onnist.'*)
oo? which person? (*'Oo said that?'*)
ooja? who do you? (*'Ere, Dave, ooja fink's gonna win the 2.40?'*)
oot a cause of merriment (*'That Craig's a right oot.'*)
oota nose
oozit who is it
oppit go away (*Oi, you, oppit.'*)
orrable not nice; hideous
ot 1) high temperature; 2) *sl* stolen

P

pacific specific
pãdda puff soft; lacking aggression (*'They're aright up front but they got a padda puff defence.'*)
pafetic miserably inadequate (*'Darren, don't be pafetic.'*)
pãfful having much power or strength (*'Craig's new motah's well pafful.'*)
pain nuisance - *shortened from* **pain in the arse** or **pain in the neck** (*'Jordan, you can be a right pain sometimes.'*)
paipa The Sun

pãnd quid (qv) *singular and plural* (*'It's only a pand to get in.'; 'That'll be twenny-five pand, guv.'*)

Pãndland a shop where nothing costs more than a pound

pãns an ãnnsis imperial weight system (*'I sell everyfink in pans an annsis – not them kilo fings.'*)

Pãnstretcher a shop where bargains might be had

pants *sl* rubbish; nonsense

parf a track for walking; pavement

peeps people; everyone (*'Aright, peeps?'*)

phat /tt/ cool

pianna

a musical instrument with strings which are struck by hammers when keys are depressed

piff white lining beneath the peel of an orange, lemon, etc

pilla a support for the head in bed

pitcher 1) an illustration; 2) pleasing to the eye (*'Oi, Trace, you look a pitcher today.'*)

plãmmans a pub lunch usually made up of cheese and bread with pickled onions, pickle and salad (*'Ere, sweetart, less go dan the juicer for a plammans.'*)

plenny an abundance (*'Thez plenny of cash in the bank, but none of it's az.'*)

pony 1) twenty five pounds sterling; 2) rubbish; useless

poota

an electronic device on which games are played

prang a slight accident in a car

proper *sl* extremely (*'That woz proper good.'*)

pukka very good; perfect (*'Thass pukka.'*)

Q

quality good (*'West Am's new striker's quality.'*)

quid pound sterling *singular and plural*

R

rager an apparatus for receiving radio signals (*'Oi, Trace, thez nuffink on the box – ennyfink on the rager?'*)

rãnd

1) a number of drinks purchased for a group of people (*'Oi Dave, ow come you never get a rand in?'*); 2) visit to a person's house (*'I'll be rand in twenny minnits.'*)

rãndeer locally *('There ain't much call for it randeer.')*

rarva 1) prefer; 2) somewhat (*'Darren, you were rarva mullered wen ya got ome last night.'*)

rat arsed *sl* drunk

Rayleigh Otter a Hollywood film actor, star of the classic *Goodfellas*

rear o' the year *sl.* idiot; *literally – prize arse*

rebãnd period of recovery and emotional turmoil after rejection by a lover (*'I couldn't elp it; I was on the reband from Craig.'*)

result a favourable outcome (*'I ad a right result on the awsses today.'*)

right naughty mischievous

rive twist about

rivvum measured flow in music, actions or speech (*'That choon that's number one's got a good rivvum.'*); **rivmic**

roofless without compassion (*'That Craig's roofless when it comes to money.'*)

S

sad /tt/ unfashionable; stupid

safe /tt/ good

sãff a direction of the compass (opp: norff)

sãffbãnd in a southerly direction

Sãffend Essex coastal resort boasting the longest pier in the world

sawted done, arranged, resolved (*'Oi, Darren, that little problem of yorn's bin sawted.'*)

sãnd what is or can be heard

sãzzman a person employed to sell goods or services (*'Ere, Darren, I got a job as a timeshare sazzman.'*)

score *sl* twenty pounds sterling

scored *sl.* was successful in one's endeavours (*'Ere Darren, I scored last night.'*)

see yer lai'er.. I look forward to meeting you again at some unspecified time in the future

seevin very angry (*'I woz seevin when I urd wot 'e sed.'*)

service industry (True story) A journalist found himself in Billericay one Sunday, passing through with his brother and girlfriend. It was about two in the afternoon and they decided to stop at a pub for a traditional Sunday lunch.

After ordering drinks, Bob asked if they served food. 'Yep,' said the ageing barman. 'Beef, lamb or turkey.'

'I don't eat meat,' said Bob. 'Do you do anything else?'

The barman tutted and said he'd have to ask the chef. Bob and his group found a table and got comfortable. A few minutes later the barman came back, stood over the table and said, 'Scampi.'

Bob and his group ordered their food and the barman left. After twenty minutes the kitchen door burst open and there stood a six-and-a-half foot tattooed skinhead with a glass eye and three plates of food. He strode over to the table, put the plates down unceremoniously, and said: 'Sixteen quid.'

customer relations

After the meal his brother took Bob's press card and announced he was going to have a bit of a laugh. He showed the card to the barman and said, 'Excuse me, we're doing a survey of pub grub in the area and I was wondering if you could give us any suggestions.'

Looking visibly shaken, the barman regained enough composure to reply: 'You don't want to eat round 'ere, mate; it's a shittol (qv).'

set me back cost. Also **set ya back, set im back, set er back** (*'It set me back a pony.'*)

shẫt

call out; speak loudly (*'Alright, Trace, yer doan 'ave t' shat in me earole.'*)

shittol *sl.* a house, town or public establishment considered to be deficient in some way

shut it please be silent (*'Oi, Jordan, shut it.'*)

shwee shall we (*'Trace, shwee go to Ibeefa again this year?'*)

simpaffy sharing or understanding an emotion or experience

skive (off) avoiding work with a false excuse (*'Oi, Dave, wot you doing ome?' 'I skived off.'*)

slater a contraction of *see yer lai'er* (qv)

smeg! an exclamation

smivareens small pieces

smoov 1) even surface; free from lumps; 2) suave (*'Eez a smoov geezer'*)

smoovee an unruffled or flattering person

smuvva overwhelm with kisses, kindness (*'Yeh aright, muvva, ya doan ave t' smuvva me.'*)

snot it is not (*'Snot much cop at Saffend in winter.'*)

snot much cop (it) is not good

snot much cop ãt there the weather is inclement

soash *sl.* social club (*'Ere, sweetart, ja fancy goan dan the soash?'*)
some /tt/ trouble (*'Ja want some?'*)
soov to calm
space cadet *sl.* a person who has plenty of space where the brain should be; a genuinely stupid person
spoze be inclined to think (*'I spoze ya wanna go dan the juicer, Darren.'*)
spoze so agreement with a degree of reluctance (*'Darren, me mum's coming rand for a bitta dinner, aright?' 'Yeh, I spoze so.'*)
srãndid has (something) to all sides (*'Craig's new place is srandid by fields'*)
stãt
strong dark beer (*'Free pints o' lager and a stat for the bald geezer'*)

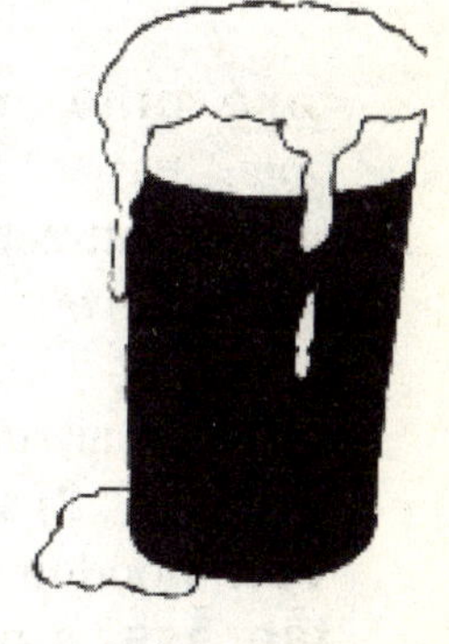

strengf the state of being strong
stension a telephone as part of a network (*'Billy the Kid and Co. Tracey speaking, wot stension do ya require?'*)
sumfing an unspecified, unknown thing (alternative spelling **sumfink**) (*'Oi, Darren, thez sumfink wrong wiv the bread pudding.'*)
summink alternative spelling of **sumfing**

sunbave

lie in the sunshine

sweetart term of endearment

T

take ome net wage (*'What's yer take ome?'*)

talent attractive members of the opposite sex (*'Dave's gone dan tan to eye up the talent.'*)

tãn 1) an urban area with a name and boundary; 2) short for tansenter

Tãn London

tãn ãss a modern terraced house, often with three storeys (*'Craig's just bort izself a tan ass.'*)

tãnsenter a place where retail therapy is available

teef plural of toof

teeving trubbles initial difficulties considered to be temporary

telepaffic communication of thoughts through extra-sensory perception

tell me abẫtt it yes, I know, I have experienced a similar situation

tevva a rope used to tie an animal

thass that is (*'Thass pukka.'*)

thez there is; there are

togevva in the company of; in conjunction with

toof one of a set in the mouth, used for biting and chewing

top evvy a woman of plentiful bosom (*'Ere, look at that, Darren; she's well top evvy.'*)

trẫnnss defeat thoroughly (*'We trannssed ya.'*)

trẫt (usually **old trẫt**) an old or ill-tempered woman (*'Shut it, you old trat.'*)

troof genuine; fact (*'I didden do it and that's the troof.'*)

trustwurvy reliable (*'Ere comes Dave in iz trustwurvy ol motah.'*)

turn rẫnnan said replied (*'...So I turn rannan said "not tonight, Darren".'*)

twenny number between 19 and 21

U

Udi Unidentified Drinking Injury. Udis are almost, but not quite, paranormal marks discovered on the morning after a night out. They usually take the form of bruises, scratches and grazes on arms or legs, from falling or walking into inanimate objects (eg. Bus stops, lampposts). Occasionally further investigation will reveal all. *('You was laying on the ground singin and some geezer tripped over ya.' 'You was dancin on top of a wall and ya fell orf.')*

ug (*usually* **a bit of an ug**) an unattractive person (*'Sharon's new geezer's a bit of an ug.'*)

ump (*usually* **the ump**) – upset. *Also* **raging ump** – well upset

undred The number between 99 and 101

ungry in need of grub

unk

a handsome chap (*'Ere, Sharon, you seen that geezer in Pandland; he's a right unk'*)

unkoof a person lacking in etiquette and manners (*'Darren, I wish you'd tell Dave not to spit at dinnertime; it's unkoof'*)

unny a term of endearment

unorfadox unconventional (*'Jordan's new mate's a bit unorfadox, innee'*)

uppill in an ascending direction (*'The new motah's alright, but it doan like going uppill'*)

urd *see* **ear** (*'Yeh, alright, Trace, I urd ya the first time'*)
urf soil
Urf

the planet on which we live
uvva not the same as something already mentioned or implied (*'On the uvva and...'*)

V

vãcher a document which can be exchanged for goods or services (*'I got a vacher to get in cheap at Forp Park'*)
vid abbrev. video (*'Bung a vid in Trace, there's nuffink on the box ternite.'*)

W

wãnnd up 1) tense (*'I'm all wannd up.'*); 2) angry; annoyed; 3) arrived finally (*'I wannd up at Pandland.'*)

waregun? where are you going?

wawazat? I beg your pardon?

webbãts in which place, specifically (*'Webbats ja live?'*)

wejja where did you (*'Oi, Darren, wejja get to last night?'*)

wejji /tt/ a practical joke whereby the waistband at the rear of the victim's underpants is grasped and pulled upwards, causing considerable but momentary pain in the nether regions

well *sl.* very (as in *well chuffed, well gutted*)

wennoff (as in *'it all wennoff'*) a fight commenced

wessbãnd in a westerly direction

wevva the atmosphere as regards temperature, rain, sunshine, wind, snow, etc (*'Wot's the wevva like?'*)

wez where is; where are

wheelbarra a small, wheeled cart used in gardening

wicked /tt/ cool; very good

wid we had; we should (*'Wid better get going, sweetart.'*)

wilya will you

wimmin plural of woman (*'Oi, Darren, thez n'arf sum fit wimmin ere tonight.'*)

windda

a glazed opening in a building or vehicle (*'Open the windda wilya.'*)

witff distance from one side to the other, usually the shorter of two lengths

wiv in the company of (*'Oi you, oppit; she's wiv me.'*)

wivvat not in the company of (*'I couldn't live wivvat yer, Trace.'*)

woancha will you not

wojja what do you (*'Wojja want?'*); what did you (*'Wojja say?'*)

wonnid 1) desired; needed 2) sought by the police

wossmatta? Is something wrong? (*'Wossmatta, Trace?'*)

wot? I beg your pardon?
wossup hello, how are you? (*'Wossup, Darren' 'Fine thank you.'*)
woz like said (in narrative) (*'So I woz like "no way" and she woz like "yeh, I ain't kiddin" and I woz like "no way" and she woz like...' etc, etc.*)
wurf value (*'He ain't wurf it, Trace.'*)

X

Y

ya the person to whom one is speaking
yafta you must; you are obliged (*'Even if yer guilty, yafta av mitigating circumstances.'*)
yoof the state of being young; 2) a young person
yoof ostall a place where holidaymakers can stay the night
yooz lot everyone present (*'Right, yooz lot, listen to this.'*)
yorn belonging to you (*'Oi, Jordan, is this stuff yorn?'*)
you wot? I beg your pardon? (*'Ere, Trace, less walk dan there for a change.' 'You wot?'*)

yuge enormous (*'Blimey, Darren, thass well yuge.'*)

Z

Zaggerate to suggest something is better or bigger than is true *('Jordan, I must've told ya a fazzund times already.' 'Don't zaggerate, mum.')*

Recipes

Estuary English is a modern dialect, so it would be out of keeping to have pages of traditional recipes. Therefore, what follows is a short selection of recipes for the modern lifestyle.

Roast dinner

What you will need:

1 car (optional)

2 microwave

Instructions

1 Go to frozen food shop and buy frozen ready meal roast dinner.

2 Put in microwave.

3 Serve

Pizza

What you will need:

1 a telephone

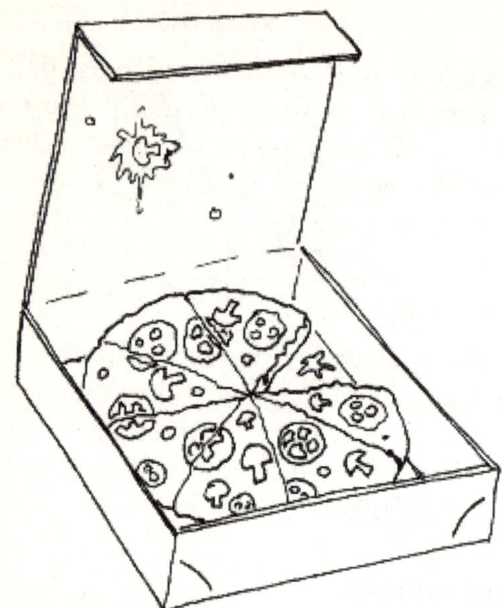

Instructions

1. Phone local pizza delivery shop.
2. Wait
3. Serve in box

Barbeque (often referred to as BBQ)

What you will need:

1 warmish day

2 barbeque grill and briquettes or similar

3 sausages and burgers

4 other stuff

Instructions

1. Set fire to barbeque briquettes
2. If no joy, squirt on some lighter fluid
3. Continue with (2) until fire catches
4. Try not to panic

5. Try water to contain fire
6. Call fire brigade
7. Wait
8. Refer to pizza recipe

Toast

This is a wonderful recipe that can be served savoury or sweet, as a snack or part of a meal.

What you will need:

1 bread

2 topping (e.g. butter, jam, cheese, chocolate and hazelnut spread)

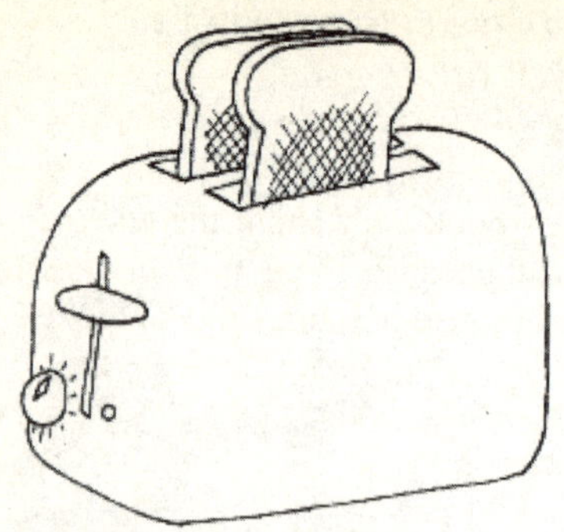

Instructions

1. Put bread in toaster
2. Wait for it to pop up
3. Spread on topping
4. Serve

Pasta

What you will need:

1 Snak Pasta pot (available in most supermarkets)
2 Boiling water

Instructions

1 Follow instructions on side of pot
2 Serve in pot

THE COCKNEY ALPHABET

The origins of the cockney alphabet date back to either Music Hall or radio shows of the 1920s. Although this book isn't about the cockney dialect, it is included because there is a connection, and also simply because it's amusing. There are several variations on most letters, particularly as this alphabet has changed over the years. For example, Esther Rantzen replaces Esther Williams, and Ivor Novello gives way to Ivor the Engine.

A for 'Orses	(Hay for horses)
B for Mutton	(Beef or mutton)
C for Miles	(See for miles)
D for Dumb	(Deaf or dumb)
E for Brick	(Heave a brick)
F for Pheasant	(Effervescence)
G for Police	(Chief of police)
H for Retirement	(Age for retirement)
I for The Engine	(Ivor the Engine)
J for Oranges	(Jaffa oranges)
K for Teria	(Cafeteria)
L for Leather	(Hell for leather)
M for Size	(Emphasise)
N for a Penny	(In for a penny)
O for The Wings Of A Dove	
P for Relief	(Glad that's out)
Q for a Bus	(Queue for a bus)
R for Mo	(Half a mo)
S for Rantzen	(Esther Rantzen)
T for Two	(Tea for two)
U for Mystic	(Euphemistic)
V for La France	(Vive la France)
W for the Winnings	(Double you for the winnings)
X for Breakfast	(Eggs for breakfast)
Y for Husband	(Wife or husband)
Z for Effect	(Said for effect)

Extra paige fer notes

The awfa would welcome yer suggestions fer entries fer the next edishun, c/o Publisher.